DIGITAL AND INFORMATION

CYBERSECURITY
PROTECTING YOUR IDENTITY AND DATA

MARY-LANE KAMBERG

rosen publishing's
rosen
central

New York

For Hope Alaimo

Published in 2018 by The Rosen Publishing Group, Inc.
29 East 21st Street, New York, NY 10010

Library of Congress Cataloging-in-Publication Data

Names: Kamberg, Mary-Lane, 1948– author.
Title: Cybersecurity : protecting your identity and data / Mary-Lane Kamberg.
Description: New York : Rosen Central, 2018. | Series: Digital and information literacy | Includes bibliographical references and index. | Audience: Grades 5–8.
Identifiers: LCCN 2017018777| ISBN 9781499439090 (library bound) | ISBN 9781499439076 (pbk.) | ISBN 9781499439083 (6 pack)
Subjects: LCSH: Computer security—Juvenile literature. | Computer networks—Security measures—Juvenile literature.
Classification: LCC QA76.9.A25 K36 2018 | DDC 005.8—dc23
LC record available at https://lccn.loc.gov/2017018777

Manufactured in China

CONTENTS

INTRODUCTION

During the December 2013 holiday shopping season, Minneapolis, Minnesota-based discount retailer Target suffered the largest cybercrime to date against a single retailer in the United States. According to the *Los Angeles Times*, the two-pronged, cyberattack affected as many as 110 million customers—a little more than one-third of the American population.

The attackers infiltrated the point-of-sale systems at 1,797 Target retail stores in the United States and 124 stores in Canada, according to *Business Insider*. Point-of-sale systems are checkout systems shoppers use by sliding their credit and debit cards to pay for purchases. The hack affected customers who used their cards in person at Target stores—but not those shopping online. With the stolen information, the criminals could fabricate cards with correct account numbers and personal information numbers (PINs). A PIN identifies a bank customer when using a credit or debit card.

Target reported on a second attack the following month. This time, the thieves were after names, addresses, phone numbers, and email addresses. The hack involved both in-store and online customers. Putting the two hacks together gave the criminals easy ways to buy things, withdraw money from bank accounts, and use the internet as if they were the actual customers. Under the false names, they could commit fraud and other crimes.

A lock icon plus "https" in a browser address bar indicates a Secure Sockets Layer (SSL) encrypted link between a web server and a browser that protects online transactions.

Businesses must be on alert for theft of customers' credit card numbers and other information. The 2013 hack cost Target $290 million, according to the international news agency Reuters.

Everyone is at risk of having personal information stolen from computers, smartphones, tablets, and other devices. Protecting equipment, personal identity, and account numbers is the job of professionals in cybersecurity. But it is not only businesses of all sizes that have to be careful nowadays. Most young people have grown up online and connected since their earliest memories. Meanwhile, their parents and grandparents spend much of their lives connected to the internet as well. Social network use, email, and other online activities, whether used via computers or ever more ubiquitous smartphones, define most people's lives. They are a primary way that people interact socially and one of the main ways that people conduct their banking and other business activities.

As everyone's day-to-day activities become increasingly digital, the possible damage that can potentially be inflicted on them by hostile and remote strangers only grows. Threats include financial crimes and cons, in addition to acts of identity theft that can ruin one's credit and reputation and even risk exposing someone to likely potential law enforcement action. Based on the practices and recommendations of professional cybersecurity experts, individuals can take steps to avoid digital intrusions and protect themselves from those who seek to compromise their privacy or steal their identities and data. Common sense, tech savvy, and constant vigilance are some of the best defenses against one of the increasingly more common crimes these days.

Chapter 1

Heroes and Villains

A mere four years after the birth of the internet in 1982, a personal computer virus originated in Pakistan and was first detected in 1986. It was called Brain. When a user put a floppy disk into an infected computer, the virus attacked the first part of the disk. Then the computer's floppy disk drive slowed down. The attack also made seven kilobytes of memory unavailable to the operating system. A byte is a unit of measurement used to describe the size of a computer's memory. A byte usually consists of eight binary digits that operate as one unit. A kilobyte equals 1,024 bytes, or 8,192 digits. Although Brain was the first PC virus, it would not be the last.

In 1989, Robert Morris created a new threat known as the Morris worm. It duplicated itself and spread so fast that it affected much of the internet, which back then had a tiny handful of users compared to today. It was the first widespread denial-of-service (DoS) attack. The goal of a DoS attack is to prevent legitimate users from accessing information or services.

For example, when a user types a URL into a browser, the user is asking a web server to view the page. In a DoS attack, the raider floods the

Before the internet was widely used, viruses were often spread via removable floppy disks, the primary tool for data storage and exchange from the 1970s through the 1990s.

network with requests. Because the server can process only a certain number of requests at once, the legitimate user can't get onto the site. According to Symantec.com, the Morris worm affected six thousand computers, about 10 percent of all computers then on the internet. When a DoS attack is waged from many different sources at once, it is known as a distributed denial of service (DDoS) attack.

Who Does This?

A hacker is a computer programmer who develops or modifies computer software to break into others' computer systems for good or ill. Some hackers try to damage the systems, shut them down, or steal personal or private information for illegal purposes. Others are skilled developers whose activities help users and businesses with computer systems.

The first hackers are believed to have appeared on the scene between 1984 and 1985 in the United Kingdom (UK). Computer users who came to be known as hackers committed a series of electronic break-ins. Among them were technology journalists Robert Schifreen and Steve Gold. They gained access to Prince Phillip's electronic mailbox in the Prestel Viewdata electronic mail service.

At the time, the UK had no laws covering computer crime. The journalists were charged and convicted of violating the Forgery and Counterfeiting Act (1981) for forging the password to gain access to the mailbox.

Their conviction was overturned on appeal. However, the event spurred parliament to enact the Computer Misuse Act in 1990.

Hackers: Wearing Many Hats

Three main types of hackers are white hat hackers (the good guys), black hat hackers (their evil twins), and gray hat hackers, who fall somewhere in between. White hat hackers know how to hack, but they use their skills for good purposes. They may participate in the free software or open-source movements that write and share software with a community of like-minded users and promote awareness of the importance of free software.

They may also help computer owners, businesses, and other organizations find and get rid of viruses. They help companies by penetration testing

In 1988, Robert Morris, a Cornell University graduate student, created the Morris worm, which caused thousands of computers to crash.

(pen testing) their computer systems to identify weak spots. If they find some, they recommend ways to strengthen them to avoid hacker attacks.

The Dark Side

Black hat hackers break into computer systems owned by banks and other companies seeking to steal money directly or to gain access to credit card information that they can sell on the black market or use to buy things for themselves.

Black hats can get hold of Social Security and bank account numbers and use them to withdraw funds or apply for credit cards in someone else's name. They can peek at medical records or learn about new products a

Discount retailer Target suffered one of the worst cybercrimes to date during the holiday season in 2013. Hackers stole credit and debit card numbers, as well as personal contact information. All told, nearly forty million customer cards were compromised.

business is developing. They can break into government data storage systems and get a look at military records and classified information.

They can also gain control of an individual's computer and blackmail the owner to restore his or her control. Or they can use their victims' computers to commit crimes that will be blamed on the innocent computer owner. Black hat hacks are crimes.

File   Edit   View   Favorites   Tools   Help

HATS OF MANY COLORS

Hats of Many Colors

Unlike white hats, black hats, and gray hat hackers, some hackers have more colorful fashion sense. Definitions vary across the internet, but here are some of the more common ones:

- Green hat hackers are the new kids on the block. They don't yet know much about hacking, but they are eager to learn. They contact other hackers and ask lots of questions in the hope of becoming proficient hackers. They are also called newbies, or n00bz in computer speak.
- Red hat hackers take the law into their own hands. If they discover a black hat hacker, they go after him or her instead of reporting the malicious activity. Red hats try to shut down black hats by uploading viruses or breaking into black hats' computers to destroy them. Red hats may also be hired by the government of one country to shut down IT systems of another country.
- Blue hat hackers seek revenge. They use some of the same techniques as red hats. The difference is their activities are aimed at getting back at a person or organization that they think has wronged them.

Gray hat hackers look for weaknesses in computer security systems but don't use them to attack for personal gain. They work without permission from the system's owner. They mostly have no malicious intent. Sometimes a gray hat contacts system owners to help them improve their security. However, sometimes the gray hat publicly releases information about the weaknesses instead of directly telling the owners. That lets black hat hackers attack the system before the company has time to fix the flaw. The damage is the same, but the spoils go to the black hat, not the gray hat.

Gray hats' activities are at best unethical. At worst they're illegal. Compromising a computer system without the owner's permission is against the law, no matter the hacker's intent.

By the time the Morris worm launched in 1989, the internet had become a vital communications tool. Users began to worry about privacy and security. This concern led to the creation of the cybersecurity industry. Cybersecurity is the collection of methods used to protect programs, data, and operating systems in computer networks, computers themselves, and other wireless devices from attack or unauthorized access. Today cybersecurity is an essential part of using technology—for businesses, governments, organizations, and individual users around the world.

Chapter 2

Viruses, Trojans, and Worms

Anyone who wants to sabotage computers, tablets, smartphones, or other devices has lots of ways to do so. Software programs designed to wreak havoc are known as malicious software—"malware" for short. The term refers to viruses, Trojan horses, worms, and spyware.

Viruses delete data or other information from a computer's hard drive. They spread over the internet. They find ways inside and change the ways computers operate without the owners knowing. Viruses run themselves, usually by piggybacking inside a file they have infected. They also duplicate themselves, which lets them spread to other computers. Damage caused by viruses includes harming programs, deleting files, or reformatting a computer's hard disk. Viruses can also take up computer memory space or result in computer crashes.

Destroy from Within

In 1995, Carl-Fredrik Neikter released the Netbus Trojan. A Trojan is a program that lets hackers gain remote access to infected computers. It looks

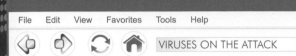

File   Edit   View   Favorites   Tools   Help

VIRUSES ON THE ATTACK

Viruses on the Attack

The five main types of viruses negatively affect computers in different ways:

- **Macro viruses** target data files. They're the most common type of virus, and they cost the most time and money to fix.
- **File infector viruses** first corrupt program files that end with .com and .exe and then spread to other files in the computer.
- **Boot sector viruses** affect the part of the hard disk used to boot—or load—an operating system. The virus activates when a user tries to start a computer that has the virus stored in its memory.
- **Record viruses** work like boot sector viruses. The difference is the way they enter the computer. Both types of viruses prevent the computer from booting up to begin with.
- **Polypartite viruses** infect both program files and boot records. If a user fixes the boot area but not the program files, these viruses again invade the boot sector.

safe, but it is an imposter. It lets hackers destroy or steal information. Unlike a virus, it can't spread by replicating itself. Instead, it must be "invited" into the computer, via an active download by the potential victim.

It is named after the famous horse that Greek soldiers hid in to secretly invade the city of Troy, according to ancient Greek myth. After Netbus, many other Trojans appeared. One affected America Online users by sending unwanted email with attachments that contained the code. When a user opened the attachment, he or she triggered the code, and it infected the computer.

Wicked Wigglers

Icons or shortcuts suddenly appear on a computer desktop. The computer runs noticeably slower. Pop-ups keep appearing. What is going on? The computer may be infected with a worm. A worm is one of the most common types of malware. It's a program that uses parts of an operating system without the user knowing it. The program continually copies itself until it uses so many resources that it slows or stops computer functions. While technically classified as a virus, a worm has different traits. The main difference is a virus needs human intervention to spread, such as running a program or opening a file. A worm spreads by itself.

A virus is one type of malicious software known as malware. Viruses damage programs and files. They can also use up computer memory space, rendering a computer hard or impossible to use.

The worm's purpose in copying itself is to spread to other computers. Worms don't need host files to duplicate themselves the way viruses do. However, they may be inserted into Word, Excel, or other documents in a way that makes the entire document, in effect, a worm. Worms send copies of themselves to other computers through email, web pages, instant messages, and other means.

Cleverly Disguised

Another kind of malware gathers data about users without them having a clue about it. It is called spyware. Spyware enters a computer through

In 2012, Hurricane Sandy knocked out power in parts of New York City, forcing many residents to get by on candlelight alone. Government officials worry that cyberattacks could cause similar outages.

suspicious and unsafe websites or email attachments. Hackers use it to steal usernames, passwords, credit card numbers, or other personal information. They also use it to track individuals' online use. Spyware is often employed for political or corporate espionage. In the private sector, hackers try to learn company secrets. Cyberspies try to gain secret, strategic information for economic, political, or military purposes. There is hardly a major power in the world that does not engage in some form of online snooping.

Another threat is adware, software that sometimes acts like spyware. However, adware is free software (sometimes called freeware) used for such benefits as toolbars, advanced searches of the internet, games, or other functions. Advertisers pay the cost of the programs in exchange for displaying ads while the programs are open. Most adware is relatively harmless, although some tends to slow down browsers and affects other software. Some adware, however, can collect information you don't want shared, such as the websites you visit. Sponsors use the information to target ads to specific users.

Gone Phishing

Phishing and botnets are other dangers lurking online. Individuals use these illegal techniques to gain information about unsuspecting computer users. Phishing is a way to trick individuals into willingly giving out personal information. The target receives an email that appears to be from a reputable business. The email requests personal information to verify their records, or some other deception. The request tricks the user into giving the information.

A botnet is a network of computers or devices that all contain malware. Criminals access these without users' knowledge and remotely control them. They use the information they get for further attacks, sending spam, or credit card fraud. Often, any one user with an infected piece of hardware has no clue of what is happening. Botnets may be idle for a while, and activated at any time by a remote server, or even nearby bots. They can be used for many purposes, including sending spam and generating DDoS attacks.

Botnets can even manipulate the infected computers (and others) into clicking on links that will generate advertising dollars for dishonest internet marketers, who may be in cahoots with the botnet's creator.

Many individuals associate cybersecurity threats only with their desktop or laptop. Yet, security risks also apply to such wireless devices as mobile phones, tablets, and gaming systems. These devices often offer the same access to unwanted invasions as computers. However, they may be even easier for the criminals, because many users fail to protect their devices with antivirus software or even enable password protection.

According to a Harris survey released in 2013, fewer than 50 percent of wireless device users protect them with passwords or PINs. And, only half of those who use mobile devices for online banking use encryption or security software. The survey also reported that fewer than 33 percent of those who use mobile devices have antivirus software on them, compared with 91 percent who have it on their computers and laptops—perhaps they don't consider the devices computers. Fortunately, security measures exist to keep users safe from unwanted hostilities.

Chapter 3

Prevention and Cure

The internet is an essential tool for business, educational research, and social connections. That is why it is important to protect computers and other wireless devices. Perhaps the most important single step is to ensure you have antivirus software, not only on computers, but also on tablets, smartphones, games, and everything else that connects to the internet. Antivirus software prevents, protects against, and removes many kinds of malware.

Antivirus software is sold by subscription by such companies as McAfee, Norton, and Microsoft. Choosing antivirus software depends on the operating system on the device and how the device is used. Gamers need different protection from that designed for email or online banking.

Internet users that are strapped for cash can also consider freeware antivirus systems, like Panda, AVG, and BitDefender. In addition, remember that many sites, especially those that engage in e-commerce or other transactions (like online banking) protect financial information while users are logged into banking profiles and other accounts. But there is no substitute

A malware attack can take users by surprise or invade without the user's knowledge. Antivirus protection prevents many different potential types of damage.

for good antivirus protection. The old adage remains true: you get what you pay for.

Check for testing and certification by such agencies as VB100%, Checkmark, ICSA Labs, AV-Test, AV-Comparatives, or NSS Labs. Free trials can help with a purchasing decision. After installation, run a security scan whenever downloading a new app or attaching a USB drive or other external device. Keep software, browsers, and operating systems current. Allow automatic updates on your devices. Updates are called patches. A patch is a piece of code designed by manufacturers to fix a bug, or problem. It can also strengthen newly discovered security weaknesses

Web Wisdom

New computers often contain add-on software, sometimes known as bloatware. Delete unnecessary programs (ones not required for the safe operation of your device). Many contain weaknesses that criminals can exploit.

Beware of links in emails, social media posts, and online advertising, even if they are believed to be from reliable sources. If anything seems odd, delete the link without opening it. Carefully consider any adware before downloading it. Ensure that the source is reputable. Be sure to read privacy agreements.

When banking or shopping online, examine URLs to be sure they start or end with an "s." Safe ones start with either "https://" or "shttp://" and contain a padlock icon. Avoid banking or shopping using Wi-Fi hotspots, accessed via cafes, libraries, hotels, and other places that offer free internet

In addition to installing antivirus programs, users can take their own common-sense security precautions when going online via Wi-Fi.

use to the public. In addition, disable your device's Bluetooth connectivity unless you're safe at home. Bluetooth uses radio waves to connect devices to each other over a short range. Unfortunately, it lets others' devices connect to yours—without your permission.

Avoid sending account numbers in emails, instant messages, or other online communications. The same goes for personal information: birth date, mother's maiden name, pet's name, or any other identifying information on social networks. Criminals can be relentless. They can

File   Edit   View   Favorites   Tools   Help

DON'T FALL FOR IT

Don't Fall for It

Scams run rampant online, so be wary of anything that seems off or too good to be true, including:

Online contests or sweepstakes that ask for payment or personal information. If you log in, use a password you don't use anywhere else.

Work-at-home offers that promise payment for reshipping goods sent to you. Investigate them online, or call to find out more information. Ask local law enforcement if specific firms are trustworthy.

Phishing scams use companies that look real—perhaps even businesses you patronize. However, their emails are fraudulent and their websites are fake. The emails often link to the "company's website," that tries to extract personal information. Instead of clicking on such links, visit the company's real website to see if they sent the message.

If you fall victim to any such cybercrimes, report them to local police, the state attorney general, and/or the Internet Crime Complaint Center (IC3). The IC3 is a partnership between the Federal Bureau of Investigation and the National White Collar Crime Center.

combine information from different sources to make educated guesses about your passwords.

In many situations, one can avoid malware infection simply by doing nothing:

- Don't download files from emails or websites you don't know.
- Don't open emails from strangers.
- Don't click on links in emails, social media, or unfamiliar websites.

Let Me In

Check new devices for default passwords included by the manufacturer. Change default ones with strong ones. And be sure to enable auto-lock on your mobile phone. Create effective passwords. Passwords should be complicated enough to make them hard to guess, even if they should be relatively easy to remember. Avoid birth dates, pets' names, or other easy-to-find personal information. Use more than six characters with a combination of capital letters, numbers, and such symbols as "&," "%," "!," or others. Try a phrase that's easy to remember, such as "Ilovebaseball" or "Pleaseletmein."

Use a different password for each site you visit. That way, criminals cracking one won't be able to use it elsewhere. Make a written list of all your passwords. Hide it where others can't find it. Avoid telling anyone your passwords—even best friends. And never save passwords on any computer but your own. It is even recommended that you avoid storing passwords with websites in general. Change your passwords often. If you receive notifications that you changed one that you know you did not, immediately contact the company in question.

Symptoms of Computer Malware

Sometimes your device is corrupted without you noticing a thing. However, many types of malware leave telltale signs:

When in doubt, consult a professional specialist for help removing malware or repairing a hard drive. At worst, even though it may be expensive, the manufacturer might be able to help.

- Error messages that your browser cannot display a web page
- A frozen or unresponsive browser
- Changed home page
- Strange or frequent pop-ups
- New toolbars
- Slow operation
- New icons on the desktop
- The control panel won't open
- Emails appear without senders or subjects

If your devices get infected, your antivirus software can probably remedy it. If not, don't try to fix it yourself unless you have lots of computer experience. Ask a trusted adult or skilled technician for aid. Consider calling in a professional. For example, Office Depot offers computer screenings. So does the Geek Squad at Best Buy stores. Other businesses and individuals provide services to clean up equipment and remove malware.

MYTHS & FACTS

MYTH Computer viruses can damage hardware.

FACT Viruses won't hurt your equipment, even if they render it useless until you figure out the problem or get rid of the viruses.

MYTH Most hackers are teenagers who cause trouble just for fun.

FACT Some hackers are sophisticated, computer savvy criminals who attack websites for such purposes as stealing information like credit card numbers for profit or to shut down the website for fun, revenge, or other reasons. Other hackers gain access to computer systems to identify and strengthen weak spots to prevent damage from outside attacks.

MYTH It's safe to meet in person someone you have met in a chat room as long as you have seen his or her photo and have a lot in common.

FACT You can never be sure who a person you meet online really is.

Chapter 4

Bad Actors

Malware is only one online peril. Identity thieves, stalkers, cyberbullies, and predators are all potential threats. Identity thieves, in particular, gain access to enough key pieces of personal information to take the place of their targets. With such information as Social Security numbers, phone numbers, birthdates, and more, the thieves impersonate the victim for a number of reasons. Imposters can even use a child's information, for instance, to sign up for credit cards, loans, and purchases with the fake name. Their crimes may not be discovered until the child comes of age and applies for credit only to learn about a negative credit rating.

At tax time, identity thieves hunt for social security numbers to file false tax returns and receive refunds. Similarly, medical identity theft has been on the rise, especially when it comes to obtaining prescription medications illegally. Other identity thieves use names, photos, and other personal information to create phony social media accounts.

The same preventive measures that protect wireless devices from malware and hacker attacks help avoid online identity theft. In addition, be

Computer users must protect their credit cards, passwords, and contact information from online thieves who seek to steal money or make purchases with the victim's money.

careful how much you share on social media. Don't give out the name of your bank or websites where you shop. The more an identity thief learns about you, the easier it is for him or her to pose as you online.

Identify Theft on Social Networks

Social identity theft often is used for cyberbullying. Bullying is unwanted, aggressive behavior aimed at harming or controlling other people or their reputation. When done online, it is cyberbullying. According to

SaveTeenRapp.org, approximately 50 percent of all youths have experienced it in some form. Cyberbullies might steal victims' identity and say or do things that imperil them, like ruining their reputation with fake posts. They may torment them with cruel or hateful language, or hack and expose embarrassing or explicit images. They may dox their victims—reveal their personal information, like their residential address, or school they attend, exposing them to further danger. Victims of cyberbullying should report it. If the bullying occurred on social media, notify site administrators. Facebook and YouTube, for instance, tend to respond seriously to complaints.

Block bullies on social media and via all other channels. If necessary, change your email address. Bullies thrive on victims' reactions. Hostile responses will only escalate a situation. Keep records of all incidents and save copies of all messages. If the situation worsens or includes threats, contact law enforcement.

Cyberbullies might reveal victims' personal information on social media to embarass or even terrorize them. Some forms of cyberbulling are crimes.

Secret "Admirers"

Cyberstalkers repeatedly use technology to frighten, threaten, and thereby intimidate victims. They send emails or instant messages, call mobile phones, or post false accusations on websites. They may also spy on victims and monitor their computer use. Cyberstalking can easily escalate to real-life stalking and even violence.

File   Edit   View   Favorites   Tools   Help

      TEENS ONLINE

Teens Online

The Polly Klaas Foundation is a national nonprofit organization dedicated to child safety that has investigated teens' online practices to identify risky behaviors. The foundation's survey of 732 minors between the ages of thirteen and eighteen found the following warning signs:

- Teens frequently communicated online with strangers via instant messaging (54 percent), email (50 percent), and chat (45 percent).
- Nearly half (42 percent) of respondents had posted personal information so others could contact them.
- More than half (56 percent) had been asked personal questions online.
- One-fourth (25 percent) had talked with someone they met online about meeting in person.
- The same number had talked about sex online with strangers, and more than one-third (37 percent) had received links to sexually explicit material.

Prevention is one good way to avoid stalkers. Googling yourself lets you see what others can learn about you. Delete personal information when you can. Delete or safeguard online datebooks that tip off others about your schedule.

If someone stalks you, save copies of all online contacts and record the date, time, and any notes about the situation. If the person's identity is known, send one clear written message that all contact is unwanted. Ignore any further contact. File a complaint with the stalker's internet service provider (ISP), as well as your own. See if yours has tools to block communications from the stalker.

Cyberstalkers may escalate their online harassment and even break the law and follow victims in person.

Report the stalker to law enforcement. Stalking is a crime throughout the United States. Take care when reporting the crime, because some stalkers can track your wireless device. You might want to change your email address and ISP. However, first check with law enforcement. The police may want you to keep these accounts open during their investigation.

Indecent Proposals

Many people encountered online are normal and upstanding. However, remember that you can never be certain who someone is, especially when the person seeks you out. Some people intentionally seek out underage victims, lying about their age and identity, and even impersonating a teenager themselves. They may seem kind and sympathetic to a teen's issues. Their ultimate goal is to establish some kind of relationship. Besides unwelcome sexual advances, such a person might mean their victims physical harm.

Use a gender-neutral screen name different from your own. Never post your age, school, phone number, address, or the name of your hometown. Refrain from filling out personal profiles or make them private. Don't admit strangers to private chats or groups, respond to their chats or instant messages, or download images they forward. Most important, never agree to meet anyone in person you don't know. If someone threatens you, tell a parent or trusted adult and report the threat to your local police.

TEN GREAT QUESTIONS
TO ASK A CYBERSECURITY EXPERT

1. Do I need antivirus protection on my mobile phone?

2. If my computer crashes, can my data files be restored?

3. If my antivirus scan shows no problems, is my device completely protected?

4. Are software updates safe?

5. How do I reach an internet service provider to block cyberstalkers?

6. Are cookies and spyware the same thing?

7. What if my antivirus program won't run?

8. How can I prevent pop-ups?

9. What is a hijacked homepage?

10. How can I remove adware?

Chapter 5

Worldwide Watchdogs

orldwide, governments suffer similar security risks, but on a larger scale. They must also be ready for cyber warfare, foreign nations' hostile use of information technology (IT). In 2003, for example, China was blamed for hacking into US military and government sites in a series of attacks dubbed Titan Rain.

Cyberterrorism is the use of technology to create widespread fear for political reasons. In 2015, a spy from Kosovo stole an online retailer's records of more than one thousand US government employees and active duty military personnel, according to *Military Times*. He turned over the names, addresses, and financial information to the Islamic State terrorist group ISIS. ISIS released the records on the internet and called for followers to use the information to commit fraud and physical attacks.

Call in the White Hats

Threats like these underscore the need for cybersecurity workers in the private, government, and military sectors. Opportunities in cybersecurity are expanding.

A cyberattack in 2013 on three banks, two broadcasters, and an internet service provider in South Korea was traced to an IP address in China but may have originated elsewhere.

According to *Forbes*, the global cybersecurity market reached $75 billion in 2015. It's expected to hit $170 billion by 2020. The US Bureau of Labor Statistics (BLS) estimates that employment of information security analysts will grow 18 percent between 2014 and 2024, higher than other occupations.

Governments will need more cybersecurity workers to protect critical information systems. So will health care providers as they expand the use of electronic medical records. Cloud services growth will also increase the demand for outsourced IT security pros. To qualify for a job in cybersecurity, an applicant needs a bachelor's degree in a computer-related field, along

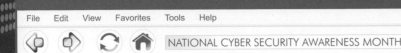

_ □ X

File   Edit   View   Favorites   Tools   Help

NATIONAL CYBER SECURITY AWARENESS MONTH

National Cyber Security Awareness Month

October is National Cyber Security Awareness Month. It's an annual, national campaign focusing on internet safety started in 2003 by the US Department of Homeland Security and the National Cyber Security Alliance. Members include government, industry, and nonprofit organizations. The campaign's purpose is to educate the public and private sectors and give them the necessary tools to stay safe online. Organizers stress the need for users to play a role in making their use of cyberspace safe, including the devices and networks they use.

with about five years of experience. Some employers prefer job seekers with a master's of business administration (MBA) that includes both business and computer courses.

Where to Study

Information security is a relatively new field, and many schools are still developing degree programs. The National Security Agency and the Department of Homeland Security have designated a number of institutions as National Centers of Academic Excellence in Information Assurance/ Cyber Defense (CAE IA/CD). Consider these schools if you want to work in cybersecurity:

- Utica College, Utica, New York
- Maryville College, St. Louis, Missouri
- Syracuse University, Syracuse, New York
- Wilmington University, New Castle, Delaware

As more schools are added, check for the CAE IA/CD designation on the institution's website. Because demand for IT security employees is so high, several organizations offer scholarships to students studying the field. They include:

- CyberCorps Scholarship for Service Program, US Office of Personnel Management
- Cisco Global Cybersecurity Scholarships
- The UMBC Cyber Scholars Program, a partnership between the University of Maryland Baltimore County/Northrup Grumman Foundation

The increasing need for workers in cybersecurity has encouraged several governments and organizations to offer scholarships for students who want to study the field.

Work experience in an IT department is also preferred, especially as a systems or network administrator or analyst. Or, employers may look for specialty experience. If the job opening is in database security, for example, the employer is likely to look for a database administrator. Industry certification is a plus. Certifications can be earned on general IT topics, as well as those specific to security.

Getting Certifications

Cybersecurity professionals who have earned professional certifications are more likely to get hired than applicants without the credentials. Several organizations offer recognized certification including:

- The Computing Technology Industry Association (CompTIA) is a nonprofit trade association providing vendor-neutral IT certifications. "Vendor neutral" means the information applies to products from many manufacturers. Their CompTIA Security+ certification validates IT security knowledge and skills. It covers essential principles for network security and risk management.
- (ISC)², an international nonprofit organization that promotes a safe and secure cyber world, offers the Certified Information Systems Security Professional (CISSP) designation. The vendor-neutral certification applies to those with proven technical and managerial skills and experience. The organization also offers certifications in cloud security, systems security, software security, health care information security, and cyber forensics. The field of forensics applies to tests and methods used in criminal investigations.
- The International Council of E-Commerce Consultants, also known as the EC-Council, offers the Certified Ethical Hacker (CEH) credential.

On the Job

Information security analysts plan and carry out measures to protect their employer's computer networks and systems. They develop security standards, and install and use such software as firewalls and data encryption that convert sensitive data into code. Security analysts monitor computer networks, watching for security breaches. If one occurs, the analysts investigate and report the extent of the damage to management. Their duties also include researching security trends, as well as recommending upgrades.

Some security analysts create disaster plans in case of emergency so they can recover information should an event destroy computers systems at its main headquarters. These analysts also test the steps in the disaster plan.

In 2015, the BLS said the median wage for information security analysts was

Job opportunities in cybersecurity include computer systems for businesses, organizations, and governments. Many cybersecurity experts work in national security.

about two-and-one-half times the national median wage for all occupations. Median wage is the middle amount earned by those in a particular job. In other words, half of workers earn more than the median wage and the other half make less. Because salary information varies and changes over time, consult the BLS online for current estimates.

Information security analysts most often work for computer companies, consulting firms, financial companies, or other businesses. They work alongside network administrators, computer systems analysts, and other IT personnel like computer and information systems managers or chief technology officers. In the chain of command, information security analysts usually report directly to upper management. In terms of hours, most positions are full time. Some employees must be on call outside business hours. In 2014, the BLS said that about 25 percent of them worked more than forty hours each week.

Stay Safe

Knowing about security risks associated with using wireless devices and connecting with the internet is an important first step in protecting yourself online. The next step is to use your devices wisely. Finally, do everything you can to avoid the dark side of the web by being aware of scams and online spies, stalkers, and predators.

Whether you're interested only in protecting yourself and your wireless devices or plan a career in cybersecurity, it pays to learn as much as you can about software and best practices to keep you safe online. Criminals are out there hacking away. Don't fall prey to them.

byte A unit of measurement used to describe amounts of computer memory.

cybersecurity A branch of security that helps users protect their computers, networks, data, and software from being accessed or harmed by others.

DDoS attack An illegal attack on a computer system with the goal of preventing legitimate users from accessing information or services by flooding a computer server with more information than it can handle so others cannot get in.

hotspots Public places where people can access the internet via a Wi-Fi signal.

identity theft A crime where someone gains access to enough key pieces of personal information about a target to impersonate the person or create a new identity with the data.

malware Short for malicious software, these are programs that are designed to wreak havoc on a target's software.

patch A piece of code designed to fix a bug, or problem, in a program or operating system. Some patches fix security weaknesses.

penetration test (pen test) An activity performed by an information security professional to identify weak spots in computer systems and recommend ways to strengthen them to avoid hacker attacks.

personal identification number (PIN) A unique identifying number that allows bank customers to access ATMs to perform banking activities.

point-of-sale (POS) systems Checkout systems where shoppers slide credit and debit cards to pay for purchases.

Trojan Short for Trojan horse, a computer virus that invades a system by obscuring its true nature from the user, such as with a digital disguise.

worm A software program that uses parts of an operating system without the computer user knowing it. The program continually copies itself until it uses so much of the computer's resources that it slows or stops computer functions.

FOR MORE INFORMATION

Canadian Cyber Incident Response Centre (CCIRC)
Public Safety Canada
National Cyber and Security Branch
340 Laurier Avenue West
Ottawa, ON K1A 0P8
Canada
(800) 830-3118
Website: https://www.publicsafety.gc.ca/cnt/ntnl-scrt/cbr-scrt/ccirc-ccric-en.
   aspx
Facebook: @GetCyberSafe
Twitter: @GetCyberSafe
CCIRC is Canada's national coordination center charged with reducing
   cyber risks for Canada's systems and services. It works with Public
   Safety Canada, as well as cities, provinces, and territories and private
   sector organizations.

Canadian Cyber Threat Exchange (CCTX)
1600 James Naismith Drive, First Floor
Ottawa, ON K1B 5N8
Canada
(613) 747-2283
Website: https://cctx.ca
Facebook: @canadian cyber threat exchange – cctx
The CCTX is a nonprofit organization that shares cybersecurity information
   with Canadian individuals and businesses. It collects and analyzes
   cyber threats and issues alerts to its members.

Center for Internet Security (CIS)
31 Tech Valley Drive, Suite 2
East Greenbush, NY 12061

(518) 266-3460
Website: https://www.cisecurity.org
Facebook: @CenterforIntSec
Twitter: @CISecurity
CIS is a nonprofit organization that develops best practices for keeping data
and systems secure. It focuses on cyber threat prevention, response,
and recovery.

Information Systems Security Association International (ISSA)
11130 Sunrise Valley Drive, Suite 350
Reston, VA 20191
(703) 234-4077
Website: http://www.issa.org
Facebook: @ISSAIntl
Twitter: @ISSAINTL
ISSA is an international organization of information security professionals. It
offers members educational forums, publications, and other opportuni-
ties aimed at improving their professional development.

International Association of Privacy Professionals (IAPP)
Pease International Tradeport
75 Rochester Avenue, Suite 4
Portsmouth, NH 03801
(603) 427-9200
Website: https://iapp.org
Facebook: @IAPPprivacypros
Twitter: @PrivacyPros
IAPP is a global organization that serves as a resource for professionals in
the IT security industry. It developed and launched the only globally
recognized credentialing programs in the field.

SANS Institute
8120 Woodmont Avenue, Suite 310
Bethesda, MD 20814
(301) 654-7267
Website: https://www.sans.org
Facebook: @sansinstitute
Twitter: @SANSInstitute
The SANS institute is a research and educational organization working to
    advance the good of the information security community.

Venus Cybersecurity Corporation
255 Centrum Boulevard, Suite 102
Ottawa, ON K1E 3W3
CANADA
(613) 696-0206
Website: http://www.venuscyber.com
Facebook: Venus Cybersecurity
Venus Cybersecurity Corporation is an international nonprofit organization
    that gives members the ability to work on cybersecurity challenges.

Websites

Because of the changing nature of internet links, Rosen Publishing has
developed an online list of websites related to the subject of this book. This
site is updated regularly. Please use this link to access the list:

http://www.rosenlinks.com/DIL/Cybersecurity

FOR FURTHER READING

Bernard, Romily. *Find Me*. New York, NY: HarperTeen, 2014.

Dalziel, Henry. *Introduction to US Cybersecurity Careers*. Waltham, MA: Syngress, 2015.

Goodman, Marc. *Future Crimes*. New York, NY: Doubleday, 2015.

Grant, Bell. *The Top 10 Cyber Careers: And What It Takes to Get One!* IT Learning Plus, 2016.

Isaacson, Walter. *The Innovators*. New York, NY: Simon and Schuster, 2014.

Lapsley, Phil. *Exploding the Phone: The Untold Story of the Teenagers and Outlaws Who Hacked Ma Bell*. Berkeley, CA: Grove Press, 2014.

Littman, Sarah. *In Case You Missed It*. New York, NY: Scholastic, 2016.

Meeuwisse, Raef. *Cybersecurity for Beginners*. Canterbury, Kent, UK: Lulu Publishing, 2015.

Rauf, Don. *Getting to Know Hackety Hack*. New York, NY: Rosen Publishing, 2015.

Schober, Scott N. *Hacked Again*. Metuchen, NJ: ScottSchober.com Publishing, 2016.

Stryker, Cole. *Hacking the Future*. New York, NY: Overlook Duckworth, 2012.

Zetter, Kim. *Countdown to Zero Day*. New York, NY: Broadway Books, 2014.

BIBLIOGRAPHY

Bestcolleges.com. "Best Online Cybersecurity Programs." Retrieved February 9, 2017. http://www.bestcolleges.com/features /top-online-bachelors-in-cybersecurity.

Connect Safely. "A Parents' Guide to Cyberbullying." July 23, 2016. http:// www.connectsafely.org/cyberbullying.

Edwards, Jim. "The Incredibly Clever Way Thieves Stole 40 Million Credit Cards From 2,000 Target Stores In A 'Black Friday' Sting." *Business Insider*, December 19, 2013. http://www.businessinsider.com /target-credit-card-hackers-2013-12.

GrayHat4Life. "7 Types of Hackers You Should Know." September 9, 2015. https://www.cybrary.it/0p3n/types-of-hackers.

Gregory, Peter H. *Getting an Information Security Job for Dummies*. Hoboken, NJ: John Wiley & Sons, 2015.

Julian, Ted. "Defining Moments in the History of Cyber-Security and the Rise of Incident Response." *Infosecurity*, December 4, 2014. https://www .infosecurity-magazine.com/opinions/the-history-of-cybersecurity.

Kamberg, Mary-Lane. *Becoming a Database Administrator* (Tech Track: Building your Career in IT). New York, NY: Rosen Publishing, 2018.

Kedmey, Dan. "Target Expects $148 Million Loss from Data Breach." *Time*, August 6, 2014. http://time.com/3086359/target-data-breach-loss.

Kovacs, Nadia. "How To Set Up and Secure Your New Tech." Norton Community, February 6, 2017. https://community.norton.com/en /blogs/norton-protection-blog/how-set-and-secure-your -new-tech?om_em_cid=hho_email_US_BLST_ACT_CLUBNORTON _2017_02.

Landesman, Mary. "Choose the Right Antivirus Software for Your PC." Lifewire.com, August 14, 2016. https://www.lifewire.com/antivirus -software-for-your-pc-152983.

McDowell, Mindi. "Understanding Denial-of-Service Attacks." US Computer Emergency Readiness Team, February 6, 2013. https://www.us-cert

.gov/ncas/tips/ST04-015.

Miller, Lawrence C. *Cybersecurity for Dummies*. Hoboken, NJ: John Wiley & Sons, 2016.

Robinson, Erin. "What Is a Computer Worm?" Product Central, October 5, 2012. http://blog.productcentral.aol.com/2012/10/05/computer -worm.

Stay Safe Online. "ID Theft, Fraud & Victims of Cybercrime." Retrieved March 28, 2017. https://staysafeonline.org/stay-safe-online /protect-your-personal-information/id-theft-and-fraud.

Stay Safe Online. "Malware and Botnets." Retrieved February 4, 2017. https://staysafeonline.org/stay-safe-online/keep-a-clean -machine/malware-and-botnets.

Symantec Corporation. "What Is the Difference Between Viruses, Worms, and Trojans?" September 30, 2016. http://www.symantec.com/docs /TECH98539.

Wharton School. "Mobile Devices and Cybercrime: Is Your Phone the Weakest Link?" June 5, 2013. Retrieved March 28, 2017. http:// knowledge.wharton.upenn.edu/article /mobile-devices-and-cybercrime-is-your-phone-the-weakest-link.

INDEX

Q

S

T

W

About the Author

Mary-Lane Kamberg is a professional writer and speaker, and author of several Rosen books about the IT industry: *Getting a Job in the IT Industry*; *Evan Williams, Biz Stone, Jack Dorsey, and Twitter*; *Becoming a Database Administrator*; and *Becoming a Network Administrator*. Her debit card was compromised in the 2013 hack on the Target retail chain.

Photo Credits

Cover, p. 1 (left to right) Georgejmclittle/Shutterstock.com, Jeff Wasserman/Shutterstock.com, deepadesigns/Shutterstock.com, Rawpixel.com/Shutterstock.com; p. 5 Marx Bruxelle/Shutterstock.com; p. 8 Adam Crowley/Photodisc/Getty Images; p. 9 Jean-Louis Atlan/Sygma/Getty Images; p. 10 George Sheldon/Shutterstock.com; p. 15 JMiks/Shutterstock.com; p. 16 Alex Fradkin/Photographer's Choice/Getty Images; p. 20 wavebreakmedia/Shutterstock.com; p. 21 m-imagephotography/iStock/Thinkstock; p. 24 Golubouvy/Shutterstock.com; p. 27 Antonio Guillem/Shutterstock.com; p. 28 AIMSTOCK/E+/Getty Images; p. 30 © iStockphoto.com/PeopleImages; p. 33 Chung Sung-Jun/Getty Images; p. 35 Phovoir/Shutterstock.com; p. 37 Echo/Juice Images/Getty Images; cover and interior pages (pixels) © iStockphoto.com/suprun.

Design: Nicole Russo-Duca; Layout: Raúl Rodriguez; Editor: Philip Wolny; Photo Research: Karen Huang